It's Nugget Time

Apostle Carla Eaddy

It's Nugget Time

Copyright ©2015 Carla Eaddy

ISBN-13: 978-0692370223

ISBN-10: 0692370226

Publishing Company

Mygazine Publications

A division of Hills Management Group LLC

3905 W. Beltline Blvd Suite 23

Columbia, South Carolina 29204

803-200-1707

Publisher's Note: This book is an original work by the author and as such, we have published the manuscript in its entirety as presented to us without additional editing for content, grammatical errors, or misspelling.

This book was printed in the United States of America

A Nugget a Day

Will Keep the Doctor Away!!!

They Are Food for Our Soul

And Healing for Our Body

Psalm 107:20

It's Nugget Time

TABLE OF CONTENTS

It's Nugget Time

DEDICATION

I want to dedicate this book to God. I give all honor to Him because He gave me the ability to do even when I thought it was impossible.

It's Nugget Time

ACKNOWLEDGEMENTS

I give thanks to my Mom, Hattie Lynch; although she was a divorcee and a single mother, she never gave up on me but yet challenged me to become the person I am. Thank you to my husband, Pastor Lewis Allen Eaddy for the role he played in my becoming an author and a writer. Thank you to my daughters; Ashley Lynch, Lt. Sierra (Mark) Lynch-Baldwin, and Delia (Odell) Bradley for provoking me to go back to college to get my degree and having the patience to help me to accomplish my dreams and goals. I want to thank my sisters; Sandra (Zebe) Johnson, Mary Robinson, Sharon Richardson, Aggie Nora (Clifton Graham) Lynch, Olivia Lynch, Tracy Lynch, Twana (Steve) Willis for playing a major role in my life and for being there for me. Thanks to my Aunt Ethel (Leroy) Wilson, Uncle Eddie (Rose) Richardson, and Aunt Marie Nettles.

I want to thank New Deliverance Faith Outreach Ministries, Second Chance Ministries, Bishop and First Lady Christopher Brown of Sword of Truth Ministries, and Apostle Laverne and Cynthia Williams of International Dream Center for provoking me to stay holy and prayerful.

Special thanks to Pastor Linda Washington, Pastor Geraldine Poole, Pastor Shirley Barr, Pastor Doris Fuller, and my God-mother Gerdline Williams. You all have been there for me all along the way. Thanks to Mygazine Publications and HMG Copy and Print Center for believing in me and publishing this book.

It's Nugget Time

CHAPTER 1

Special Nuggets

It's Nugget Time

Don't You Get It?

You Were Created And Designed To Win.

Special: Yea though they slay me, Yet will I trust (Job 13:15)

Special: How long will you allow what's inside of you to be hidden and not used?

Special: The test isn't if you fail, it's what you do with the power inside of you.

Special: According to Isaiah 43, aren't you his? (O Israel, Fear not: for I have redeemed thee, I have called thee by thy name; thou art mine)

Special: Doesn't he say that the water shall not overtake you and that you can walk through the fire and not be burnt? (Isaiah 43:2)

Special: Who else can give you the OK to GO THRUUUU the water and fire and be absolutely sure you will and not die but live and declare the works of the Lord.(Psalms 118:17)

Special: There is nothing that God hasn't thought of when it concerns His love for you.

Special: So get up! ARISE! SHINE! SHAKE YOURSELF! SURE YOU COULD BE EXHAUSTED!!!

Special: BUT YOU STILL WIN! KEEP PUSHING! YOU WANT CHANGE? CHANGE YOUR THINKING!

Special: YOU'VE ALREADY WON! YOU HAVE ALREADY BEEN REDEEMED!

Special: STRIVE AND GO FORTH... YOU'VE GOT THIS!

Special: PUSH...YOU'VE GOT THIS!!! YOU ARE A WINNER!!!!

Don't Die In The Valley

Special: Don't Means: do not

Special: Die Means: Stop living: to cease to be alive.

Special: In Means: (used to indicate inclusion within space, a place, or limits): walking in the park.

Special: Valley Means: Low-lying area: a long low area of land, often with a river or stream running through it that is surrounded by higher ground.

Special: The valley is place where God take us, so He can mature us and make us into that person that he has design from the being of time. It's down in the valley where we must learn how to survive by trusting in the one that has allowed us to be in the valley. There is time in our lives where things will raise up and it will seem like death, but it's only the shadow of death that will bring fear and doubt into our life. To us think that life is not worth live, it will help you in your spiritual growth with God and it will push you into the level that God has design for your life!!!

Seasons Do Change!!

Special: Season Means: each of the four division of the year (Spring, Summer, Autumn , and Winter) marked by particular weather patterns and daylight hours, resulting from the earth's changing position with regard to the sun.

Special: Do Means: to perform (an act, duty, role, etc.)

Special: Change Means: make or become different (someone or something) different.

Special: This is what God is saying, this season is special!

Special: Seasons do change!!

Special: God is saying that seasons do change! No matter what you are facing with in life situation. It will change when you allowed it to change! But it will change for the best!!

Special: Allow God to change your situation and your life in this new season!!

Special: Daniel 2:21

Chapter 2

Drop Nuggets

It's Nugget Time

To Fall Or Let Fall In Drops
[Tears Dropped From Eyes.]

Drop: Nugget Means: A lump or rough piece: especially, a lump of gold ore.

Drop: God gave me this word a few days ago for his people, and I had to wait on the revelation from my Heavenly Father. This is what God is saying, in this season, is that he have allowed so many people to come and go, in and out of our lives whether they were negative or positive for a purpose to **DROP**.

Drop: Endurance is in our lives to help us make it through life's journey that HE has set or has had planned for our life. We will make it through no matter what we have.

Drop: What situations that we have faced on this life's journey

Drop: Nothing but tears that God has allowed to fall from the many issues that we had to go through in our lives. Let a lump or a rough piece of a nugget become a Lump Of Gold that he can use for his glory.

Drop: God allowed you to drop to help design and develop you to become into that awesome Man or Woman of God that God was making for his Glory.

Drop: Sometimes there are rough pieces in all kinds of lumps, but by the time it comes into its fullest form or a nugget has been through something it can be that rare piece of gold.

Drop: Be a great value to the jewelers that are willing to pay higher price for gold. That will give them return on their investment.

Drop: I will make a man more precious than fine gold.(Isaiah 13:12)

This Is Your Season For Greatness !!

Drop: I Hear God Said Mega Millions Shall Flow Into Your Life!! Your Investment Shall Return A 100 Fold Blessing!!!

This Is Your Nugget From Ecclesiastes 11:1:10

From: The Apostle Desk

You My Baby!!

Drop: God said within the next few days you are getting ready to experience that new fresh "Fire Anointing" that will destroy the works of the enemy dead in his tracks he has for you. When the consuming fire comes that's when true healing and deliverance can take place like never before!! This is the season for the "Two Fold Blessing" to take place. The "Double, Double Blessing, $7 + 7 = 14$" The seven has now connected together!!! From the mouth of God!!

Isaiah 61:7

Just hold on....Keep PUSHING! GTEATER IS COMING!

Drop: Waiting with great expectations. Birthing pains will produce if we faint not. Keep looking for our redemption draws near. We serve a Great God who has never failed us yet and wont. We rejoice today because of Him. On your job shine for Him and know no weapon that is formed against you shall prosper. Love you!!!

THE MOMENT WHEN YOU WANT TO QUIT, IS THE MOMENT WHEN YOU NEED TO KEEP PUSHING.

Amen!! ...Keep On Rolling!!

Drop: There comes a time in our life or our walk with God that we will be tested or confronted with several different types of storms or circumstances in our life or in our season!!!

Drop: We must learn how to keep on rolling in the midst of the storms or circumstances that will come our way!!!

Drop: So that we can get to the other side of your storms or your circumstance!!

Drop: The storms only come to increase our faith and to help us to become more mature in the things of God containing the will of God for our life!

Drop: We must stay focus at all time, when we are in our storm or our circumstances while going through our storm!!!!

Drop: God told me to tell you, that you have the power to control your storms or circumstances that comes up in your life!!

Drop: Encourage somebody by telling them today to keep on rolling!

Drop: Just remember this key nugget: If you keep rolling you be on the other side before you know it!!

Drop: There is victory in your rolling!! So just get to the other side and claim your victory today!!

Mark 5:1

Waiting With Great Expectations

Drop: Birthing pains will produce if we faint not. Keep looking for our redemption draws near. We serve a Great God who has never failed us yet and wont. We rejoice today because of Him. On your job shine for Him and know no weapon that is formed against you shall prosper.

Love you!!!

For Forgiveness Is The Places Of Healing.

Drop: Let healing process take place. So you can walk free.

Drop: Tell somebody or anybody just for forgiveness!

Drop: Forgiveness will bring a healing heart and a happy heart, with a peace of mind! Try it you will love it!!

The Two Fold Blessing

Drop: The means: denoting one or more people or things already mentioned or assumed to be common knowledge.

"What's the matter?

Drop: Two means: equivalent to the sum of one and one; one less than three;

"Two years ago"

Drop: Fold Means: bend (something flexible and relatively flat) over on itself so that one part of it covers another.

Drop: Blessing Means: God's favor and protection.

"May God continue to give us his blessing"

Synonyms- protections, favor: "May God give us his

Blessing"

Drop: My children, God said within the next few days, you are getting ready to experience the new, fresh, fire anointing that He has for you, will destroy the work of the enemy-dead in his tracks. When the consuming fire comes, it will bring true healing. True deliverance will take place in our lives like never before.

Drop: In this season it will bring a two-fold blessing that will take place that is called the double, double blessing.

Drop: This is how you get the two-fold blessing. $7+7=14$. The sevens have now connected together and it will bring the two-fold blessing or the double, double blessing in this season.

Drop: From the mouth of God, Isiah 61:7.

It's Nugget Time

Chapter 3

Fire Nuggets

Don't Die In Your Mess!

Fire: "Don't" means contraction for do not. "They really don't know what will happen"

Fire: "Died" definition is death of a person, animal, or plant stop living. "She died of cancer"

Fire: "In" means the chemical element indium.

Fire: "Your" is used to refer to the person or people that the speaker is addressing. "Are you listening?"

Fire: "Mess" is a situation or state of affairs that is confused or full of difficulties. "The economy is still in a terrible mess" Plight, predicament, tight spot/corner, difficulty, trouble, quandary, dilemma, problem, muddle, mix-up, imbroglio; informal jam, fix, pickle, stew, scrape "I've got to get out of this mess"

Fire: What "God" is saying in this season is that He doesn't want anyone to die in their mess. He has greater things in store for you in your life. He wants to show you off to the world. God is calling you out of darkness into his marvels light, so he can use you for his glory!! You have been in your mess too long; God has his eyes on you for His divine purpose. God is saying, now is the time. Don't allow this moment to pass you by because of the pain, hurt, and disappointed that you have had to endure in your life at an early age, even up until now!!!!! God wants to be the easer of your past, He can push you into your destiny that he has already created for you from the foundation of the world.

Fire: He said come unto me, he that heavy laden and he will give you the rest that you need at this time in your life!!! God loves us so much that he does not want us to die in our mess, but show us his love that he has for us, even when we mess up on him!! Just remember, if you are a "Backslider," He is waiting for you with his arms wide open!!! God's Love for You!

Hot Hot Hot

Fire: Do you understand the power of a renewed mind, changed mind, a mind that is focused on the promise and not the process. Don't become spoiled by your own attitude....

Be Encouraged Today!

Fire: CLAIM IT! Its already getting better, its already getting easier! GOD DID IT! Yes God did it for me! PRAISE GOD! ONE DAY CLOSER TO THE PROMISE!

Let The Glory Of The LORD Rise Upon You!!

From The Apostle Desk!!

Chapter 4

Nugget Time

It's Nugget Time

The Fake Or The Real Ones!!!

Time: There comes a time in life when the rubber meets the road.

This is one of these times when you will learn fake people from the real people, whether it be family, friends or whomever.

Time: How Will You Know Them A Part!

Time: 1.The Fake One Will Always Live In The Past.

Time: 2. The Real One Will Always Live In Your Future!!

Are You Ready For Your Jubilee Blessing?

Time: God spoke to my spirit and said this is the year of the great JUBILEE which means a celebration for the GREAT I AM.

Time: Which means he's giving every lost soul a chance to come and reign with him and a chance to repent for all the remission of their sins.

Time: In this year spiritually gifts will be unleashed and made manifested boldly in his chosen people.

Time: This is definitely the year of THE GREAT JUBILEE THE GREAT I AM!!!!

Time: From the Mouth of God!!

Stop Chasing Waterfalls!

Time: Something to ponder... How much time have you wasted chasing or attaching yourself to MISTAKEN IDENTITIES?

Time: God never said you were nobody, a has been, a good for nothing. When did he tell you cancer belong to you or this is your high blood pressure or your diabetes?

Time: Sometimes you can be the victim so long that you began to play the part even when you're wrong.

Time: Why are we so quick to receive and believe the lies of the enemy? Who told you that you were naked Adam?

Time:: God created us in his own image STOP standing in the mirror trying to ADD something to his Image.

Time: Don't you get it, YOU ARE... BECAUSE HE IS...Now Beloved ARISE! SHAKE THE DUST OFF!

Time: GET BACK UP! FOR YOUR LIGHT ISSSSS COME. IT'S TIME TO LIVE! WHY YOU TRYING TO DIE?

Time: Stop chasing water falls don't you get it? It FALLS. Nugget: So don't allow people, Doctors, teachers, or anyone to speak a MISTAKEN IDENTITY over your life.

Time: Sure the fact maybe your blood is high pressure but we are ONLY concerned with HIS TRUTH YOU'RE HEALED! Fresh Manna Flowing Down From Heaven!! IT'S RAINING, Can You See, Hear or Feel!!!!!

Time: There Comes A Time When We Must Stop Chasing Negative Things , Thoughts, People, Dreams And Begin To Do It God's Way, For Positive Results In Our Lives.

The Nugget for this Season is Agape (Love and Forgiveness)

Allow God to heal you from the inside out. God is looking for the people that don't mind being transformed from inside out. (GOD GREASTEST GIFT TO YOU IN THIS SEASON...

Remember That Time Is So Powerful

It Will Help You Stay Focus On What Is The Most Important Things And People In Your Life. Then You Can Keep On Moving Forward!! Love Will Always Run Deep!!!!!

Prayer of Repentance

God is calling his people back to him with an Inner man (THE SOUL MAN) Repentance! Not Outside in, but, the Inside Out. It's time to EXHALE; Not Waiting to EXHALE, the waiting period is over.

The Heart of Thanksgiving

First of all I would like to thank God for allowing his blessing of thanksgiving too shine upon my family, my friends, in spite of some of our major loses that we endured this year! Just remember it's not about you. It's about giving thanks to God and helping someone that is less unfortunate then you are!!! (To Share Plate, Is To Share Or Show Some Love)

Wasted Time

Time: Wasted Mean: To Use Up Or Spend Without Real Purpose; Make Bad Use Of [Waste Money Or Time.]

Time: Time Mean: The Period Between Two Events Or During Which Something Exists, Happens, Etc.

Time: We Are Living In A Time Where We Must Enjoy Every Moment, Because We Don't Know What Tomorrow Will Bring Our Way!!!! So Stop Wasting Time And Live Your Life Like You Have Purpose!!!!!

Time is like a river.
you cannot touch the same water twice,
because the flow that has passed will never
pass again.
Enjoy every moment of life....

Walk By Faith

Time: Walk means - To move along on foot at a normal speed [Walk; do not run, to the nearest exit.]

Time: By means - near or beside [Sit by the Fire]

Time: Faith means - belief or trust that does not question or ask for proof (Job kept his faith in spite of his troubles.)

Time: There comes a time in life, that you must learn how to walk in the faith realm so you can receive the awesome blessings of God, because you realize that you can't touch it or see it, but you know that it's there when you look through the eyes of God you can see it.

2 Corinthians 5:7

Wasted Plan

Time: Remember wasted time or plan is not in the will of God.

Time: Wasted means: To use up or spend without real need or purpose, make bad use of (To Waste Money or Time).

Time: Plan Mean: A method...or way of doing something that has been through out ahead of time (A Plan of the Battlefield).

Time: Time Mean: The passing hours, days, years, etc: every moment there has ever been or ever will be (Time and tide wait for no man.)

Time: As I waited for God to speak into my inner man about this word that he gave me yesterday, for today into ears of the heart, of the inner man.

Time: Wasted Plans are the plans that we have set for our own life, on our own, that doesn't have anything to do with the "Master Plan". So when it does have anything to do with the master plan that God has already set for us it brings lots of heartaches and pain into our life.

Time: Jeremiah: 29:10:11

Wasted Talent

Time: Wasted means: used or expended carelessly, extravagantly, or to no purpose. "Wasted fuel" squandered, misspent, misdirected, misused, and dissipated; pointless, useless, needless, unnecessary; vain.

Time: Time means: plan, schedule, or arrange when (something) should happen or be done. "The first track race is timed for 11:15" Schedule, set, set up, arrange, organize, coordinate, fix, line up, slot in, prearrange, timetable, plan; slate. "The events were timed perfectly"

Time: I waited for God to speak to me about this word that he gave me a few days ago about Wasted Talent. God has given us these talents from the foundation of the world for the use of his glory. God is saying when people don't use their talents or gifts that he design for then to use it, then it became wasted. Then it could cause people a lot of pain and disappointment in their life, because they begin to waste the very thing that would have made them successful or wealthy in their life. So when we don't walk the plan that, God has set for our life then we misuse or mishandled the talent or gift that God has designed to be used for His glory. Then we walk around life with no purpose for our lives. So we are being to waste away the real meaning for our talent and life.

Time: God wants us to give him back the talent or gift that was given to us from the foundation of the world, so he can show off his glory through the use of our talent or gift. We just got to submit our talent and gift back to the very one that entrusted us to use it.

Time: Just remember that the talent that God has given unto us is for us to bring glory to his name and to give increase with us. I'm reminded about the story in the book of Matthew where God begin to give out the talent to them, and after a while God came back to see if they had done anything or brought an increase with the talent that he had entrusted them with. When he saw that the man wasted or buried it, and then he took it from him and added to the other man talent, because they didn't waste it. So! You can use it or lose it!!!!

Time: And unto one he gave five talents, to another two, and to another one; to every man according to his several ability; and straightway took his journey.

Matthew 25:15

God Is On My Side!

Time: God Means: Is the all- powerful being who made and rules the universe and worshiped by man.

Time: Is Means: the form out of be showing the present time with singular nouns and with he, she or it.

Time: On Means: held up by, covering, or attached to (a pack on his back).

Time: My Means: of me or done by me: the possessive form I , used before a noun and through of as adjective (my God)

Time: Side Means: the position beside one (He Never Left My Side.)

Time: There comes a time in life that we must understand that if God wasn't on our side the enemy would have taken us out before now. But God in a bad situation. Thank you Lord for being on our side!

Time: Psalms 124:1-8

I am perfect in my imperfection, Happy in my pain, Strong in my weakness & beautiful in my own way, because God is on my side ! ＼ツ／

You Can't Kill A Dreamer!

Time: There are always somebody that wants to kill the dreamer because of the dreams that God had entrusted you with from the foundation of the world!!

Time: Because they are jealous of your dreams that God has given unto you!!

Time: Just remember your dreams will bring you before great kings and queens!

Time: You must understand that when you share your dream, they will try to destroy you, because of that dream that you reveal to them!

Time: So be careful who you reveal your dreams to!

Time: Remember! Because Joseph revealed his dreams and his brothers meant to destroy him!

Time: They meant it for evil, but God meant it for his good!

Time: It's going to pay off in the long run!

Time: Genesis 50:20

It's Time!

Time: This is your season to reap what you have seed!

Time: All the hell that you have to go through was to help design you for where God has taken you in this season!!

Time: For your double blessing that God had special design. You and all those that push you into that wealthy place!!

Time: This is your season of recovery!!

Time: 1 Samuel 30:8

Just Say Amen

Time: Just Means: That is right or fair [a just decision; just praise].

Time: Say Means: To speak or pronounce; utter [" hello, he said,]

Time: Amen Means: a Hebrew word meaning "may it be so!" or "so it is": used after a prayer or to express approval.

Time: There comes a time in our life or walk with Christ that we must come into an agreement with God's word and our life situation!! So we can move forward in the things that God has for our life, as well as our future. When you say Amen, you are telling God that you agree with whatever his word said about your life and that you are willing to accept him at his word!!!

Time: Even when the word finds us in places that may not be comfortable, if we just agree with it!! It can change your life forever!! "Just One word"

Victory In One Place
But Hell In Another Place!

Time: There are times in our lives when we have victory in one area, but hell in another area of your life.

Time: God is saying that he has everything in control that comes into your life.

Time: So no matter what goes on in your life just continue standing on the word of God!

Time: Because he will give you victory over other circumstances that you are dealing with in your life.

Time: Remember he is God! He knows all and sees all!

Time: That's why you can have victory in one area of and hell in another because he's able to give you victory again.

Time: Remember if he did it before he can do it again!

Time: 1 Samuel 30:8

When I See The Hand Of God Move!!

Time: Have you ever been in a situation, where you needed to see the hand of God move!!

Time: My hand in now moving on your behalf, so the enemies can see it.

Time: God said step back because he does want you to get your hands dirty!!!

Time: God in this season keep your hand clean!!

Time: Only them that has clean hands and a pure heart will inherit the things of God!!

Time: Let us stay focus on the move of God that's going to bring victory over our circumstance!!

Time: 2 Chronicle 20:17

Unexpected Blessing
Will Come In This Season!!

Time: I hear God saying that's how our blessings are going to come unexpected in this season!

Time: It does seem like the blessing is going to happen, but it will!

Time: Because of the many obstacle that will try and get in the way!!

Time: Remember to expect the unexpected in this season!

Time: Unexpected is that uncommon blessing that make no sense at all!!!

Time: 2 Kings 7:2

Humbly Bowed

Inner Healing of My Soul

Time: Soul means: The immaterial essence, animating principle, or actuating cause of any individual life. The spiritual principle embodied in human beings, all rational hand spiritual beings, or the universe

Capitalized Christian Science:

    (a) GOD

    (b) a person's total self

    (c) any active or essential part

    (d) a moving spirit: LEADER

Don't Allow Your "It" To Kill You!!!

Time: God is saying whatever your "It" is. Don't allow it to take you out in this season or stop your blessing.

Time: You are the only one who knows what your issue is. Whether it is money, friends, men, women, children, a job, etc… Don't let everything depend on your actions, whether it be good or bad!!

Time: It's up to you to cut it off or God will!! Don't allow anything to stop, or cut off your blessing in your season!

Time: God said for the next seven years we will operate in the double blessings!!

Time: We must stay in right standing with God for us to attain these blessing of promise!!

Time: 2 King 7:4

This Special Day: The King's Day!! (Jesus)

He is saying the King is here, this is the best day that you can read your heart and not your garments. (Joel 2:13) The Great Gift you can give the birthday man knows...

GOD WILL DO IT AGAIN!!!!

Time: Glory Means:
1) a state of great gratification or exaltation.
2) Praise, or distinction extended by common consent: renown.
3) A height of prosperity or achievement.
4) The splendor and beatific happiness of heaven; broadly:

eternity.

Time: GOD IS LOOKING FOR SOMEOME THAT HE CAN SHOW OFF HIS GLORY.

Time: Revelation: 7:12

Just Praise God!!!

Time: To God be the glory for who he is for all the great things that he has done and still doing for you in the season!!! As we are getting ready to exit out of our old season, and enter into our new season, just give God praise!!!! Praise your way out and into the next season!!! All praise, glory and honor belongs to him!!

Hallelujah!!!!!!

It's Nugget Time

Chapter 5

Super Sunday

Nuggets

It's Nugget Time

Remain Steadfast In The Faith!

Super Sunday: Blessed is the man who remains steadfast under trial, for when he has stood the test. He will receive the crown of life, which God has promised to those who love him.

James 1:12

Holding On To The Promise Of God!!

Super Sunday: There comes a time in your life when it seems impossible to keep on going in the things on God!!!

Super Sunday: It seems like all odds are against you, but its only God trying to get you to the land of promise!

Super Sunday: Remember it will cost you everything that you have, to attain the promise that God has design for you!!

Super Sunday: It won't be easy, because it's designed to make you ready for what has for you in this land of promise!!!

Super Sunday: Remember! It cost the children of Israel some heartache and pain, because they want to do it their way!!!

Super Sunday: Remember! It's time to reach your land of promise that God has promise and show you!!

Super Sunday: Don't give up on the promise of God and don't allowed peoples to make you miss your land of promise!!

Super Sunday: Just keep the faith and your focus on your promise land!!!!!

Super Sunday: Joshua 1:6

Let God Do It!!

Super Sunday: There comes a time when we will have to let God do it for us!

Super Sunday: When you take the time to look back over your life, then you can see that only God could have done it!!!

Super Sunday: It is God that is able to take care of us and make things happen in our life!!

Super Sunday: Sometimes we are too busy trying to do it ourselves and find ourselves in distress!!

Super Sunday: The reason for that is because we don't trust God, so we find ourselves playing God, instead of allowing God to just do it!!!!

Super Sunday: God want us to know that he is able to take care of his people!!

Super Sunday: Remember! If God takes care the fowl of the air surely he can take care of us!!!!

Super Sunday: Luke 12:22:31

~Humbly Bowed~

Got To Have Peace!!

Super Sunday: Pursue peace with all people and holiness, without which no one will see the Lord:

Super Sunday: Look carefully lest anyone fall short of the grace of God

Super Sunday: Lest any root of bitterness spring up cause trouble, and by this many become defiled;

Super Sunday: Lest there be any fornicator or profane person like Esau, who for one morsel of food sold his birthright.

Super Sunday: For you know that afterward, when he wanted to inherit the blessing, he was rejected, for he found no place for repentance!

Super Sunday: Thought he sought it diligently with tears.

Super Sunday: As the body of Christ, we are urged to pursue peace and holiness together.

Super Sunday: These are things that cannot be achieved without love, forgiveness, correction, and hearts that are willing to change.

Super Sunday: The enemies to this cause are bitterness, resentment, anger, hate, division, envy, greed, etc.

Super Sunday: Ultimately, our enemy is idolatry, and many times it is our own self that serves as our largest stumbling block.

Super Sunday: The challenge is to set aside your own interests, and replace that effort toward the good of others in Christ Jesus.

Super Sunday: You need to do what Esau could not.

Super Sunday: He could not see straight in the face of hunger, and sold his birthright to his younger brother for a meal on a whim.

Super Sunday: His birthright was worth much more, yet He could not make the choice that reflected that truth.

Super Sunday: What drives your choices?

Super Sunday: Love, self, or something else?

Super Sunday: Hebrews 12:14-17

~Humbly Bowed~

It's Victory In Your Praise

Super Sunday: When you are going through life troubles, just begin to give God a praise!

Super Sunday: Your praise is a weapon that you must know how to utilize in the mist of your battle!

Super Sunday: It's your praise that will defend your enemies!!

Super Sunday: Remember! Praise is what we do when we are going through!!

Super Sunday: It's your praise that moves the hand of God, not your crying and complaining!!

Super Sunday: So wake up each day with a praise in your heart and on your lips.

Super Sunday: Ps 34:1

Tried By Your Faith!

Super Sunday: It's not the devil testing you, its God trying you!

Super Sunday: God wants to get the glory out of our life!!

Super Sunday: If you just trust God while you going through your faith test!

Super Sunday: He will give you the grace to overcome the tests that he have allow to come your way!

Super Sunday: God has allowed you to go through the fire to mature you faith!

Super Sunday: He gave his hardest battles to the strongest soldiers!

Super Sunday: So know that you already have the victory over the enemies!

There will always be trails and tribulation to produce perseverance, character, and hope.

Romans 5:3-5

The Blood Still Work!

While in 5:00 am prayer the Lord began to speak about the blood of Jesus! God said that my blood still works for my people! Whatever you need is in the blood of Jesus Christ, whether it may be healing, deliverance, salvation! The blood that cover a multitude of sin, no matter what it is!!!!!! Remember the blood will never lose its power, it will reach the highest mountain, and it will flows to the lowest valley.

"Stay under the blood of Jesus"

1 John 1:7

Silent Is Not An Option!

There comes a time when the children of God can no long be silent! When it comes down to telling people about the goodness of Jesus!! We are living in a time where we must begin to cried loud, so that soul can be save!! When we keep silent it allow the enemies to kill, steal and destroy lives!! It's out duty or job to win souls for the kingdom of God!! We must share our story about how Jesus has transformed our life!!

~Humbly Bowed~

Whole Armor!

Remember, our goal in spiritual warfare is to stand firm in our faith in Christ Jesus. The enemy would have you doubt the truth of God, just like he did with Adam and Eve in The Garden of Eden. (Genesis 3) Because of Christ we are able to "put on" salvation, faith, truth, righteousness, and the gospel of peace as armor. These are very real and they protect us along with the word of God (our offensive weapon). Each of these things are gifts from God through belief in and fellowship with Christ. Ask God to help you suit up for what is in store. You have help, protection, and are never alone in Christ.

Ephesians 6:13:17

~ Humbly Bowed ~

Just Embrace!!

Super Sunday: Now that the change has come, you must now embrace the change!!!!

Super Sunday: It's important to allow God to change our lives, so we can walk into our over flow blessings that God has for his people.

Super Sunday: When you embrace it, then the changes will take places!!

Super Sunday: Remember that change is will never be easy, but it is necessary!!

Super Sunday: God can change our lives in a way that people couldn't even imagine!

Super Sunday: So embrace the change that God has for you today!!

Super Sunday: Job 14:14

~Humbly Bowed~

Five P's Prayer, Process, Press, Push, Praise

Super Sunday: We are in season where we must operate in the Five 'P's, Prayer, Process, Press, Push, Praise.

Super Sunday: Prayer is the number one 'P', because we must have a prayer life like never before!! We must always have our weapon of prayer at all time!!

Super Sunday: Process is the second 'P', because we must go through our process that God has design for our lives and we must trust him with the outcome.

Super Sunday: Press is the third 'P', because we must be willing to "Press" beyond our flesh and our feeling so we can get the healing that we need to do God will!!!!

Super Sunday: Push is the fourth 'P', because once you have started to "Press" then you will need to continue to push your way through any situation that come your way!

Super Sunday: Praise is your fifth "P", because you will always need your weapon of "Praise" to fight your battle for you.

Super Sunday: We must be like the woman with the issue of blood that had to go through the five step of the 'P's for a moment with Jesus to receive her total deliverance and her healing!!!

Super Sunday: Mark 5:25:34

~Humbly Bowed~

Apostle Carla Eaddy

Chapter 6

Super Monday

Nuggets

It's Nugget Time

Letting Go Of The Wrong People Will Hurt, But Embracing The Right People Will Be Much More Beneficial To Your Life!!

Super Monday: Remember God cares about the people you allow to come into your life!!

Super Monday: So trust God, when it comes to letting people go!!! You won't be disappointed!!

~Humbly Bowed~

Promotion Come Through The Fire!

When you learn how to go through the fire then you can get your promotion!! The fire won't consume you or burn you, because God will cover you in the mist of the fire!! It's just to bring you to a place of wealth!! If God delivered Daniel out of the lion's den and Hebrew men through the fire, he will bring you through your fire!!!

Isaiah 42:2

~ Humbly Bowed

Don't Cry Just Push!

Super Monday: What you're crying about now, you will be shouting about later!!

Super Monday: Don't you dare get discouraged!

Super Monday: God is shaking you so you can get rid of what does not belong!

Super Monday: So that your next will be more effective than your now!!

Super Monday: The baby has turned in your belly. Get ready!

Super Monday: It's Time To Deliver!

Super Monday: Keep Pushing! Keep Pushing! Keep Pushing!

Super Monday: Love your midwife who loves you more!

Super Monday: The baby has already turned. You are long overdue.

Super Monday: God has induced labor, push! It's time to push ... Now!

Super Monday: Don't miss your moment to deliver your purpose!!

~Humbly Bowed~

My God

Super Monday: My God shall supply all my need according to his riches in glory in Christ Jesus.

Super Monday: My God is able to do the impossible, no matter what the situation look like in our life!!

Super Monday: He will supply all of our needs, only if we obey his word!!!

Super Monday: Philippians 4:19

~Humbly Bowed ~

We Need Your Glory Lord!!

Super Monday: We need to be hungry for God's glory!

Super Monday: We are in a season where you have to be!

Super Monday: Hungry for the Glory of God!!

Super Monday: We will need God's Glory to survive in 2015 because without God's Glory you will be fighting a losing battle!!

Super Monday: We shouldn't want to be in a place where glory cannot be!!

Super Monday: Because of where God's Glory are miracles and healing take place!!

Super Monday: Where the Glory Of God is there is victory! Glory!

Super Monday: Isaiah 1:6

~Humbly Bowed~

Are There Any Je·hosh·a·phat Out There?

I hear The Lord said, "Ye shall not need to fight in this battle; set yourselves, stand ye still, and see the salvation of The Lord with you. O Judah and Jerusalem fear not, nor be dismayed; tomorrow go out against them; The Lord will be with you.

2 Chronicles 20: 17

Fight The Battle That Come Your Way That Was Design To Destroy You And Make You Stop Trusting In Your God.

~Humbly Bowed~

It's Nugget Time

Chapter 7

Super Tuesday
Nuggets

It's Nugget Time

Change

Super Tuesday: It's hardest on those who have difficulty changing.

Super Tuesday: Not new, but change is important. We must expect change when it comes our way!

Super Tuesday: Never easy, but it's a process that we must allow to take place in our everyday walk with Jesus Christ!!!!

Super Tuesday: It will make the different in our life!!

~ Humbly Bowed~

Just Be Content!

Super Tuesday: Not that I speak in respect of want

Super Tuesday: For I have learned, in whatsoever state I am, therewith to be content

Super Tuesday: I know both how to be abased, and I know how to abound:

Super Tuesday: Everywhere and in all things I am instructed both to be full and to be hungry, both to abound and to suffer need.

Super Tuesday: I can do all things through Christ which strengthens me.

Super Tuesday: Notwithstanding ye have well done, that ye did communicate with my affliction.

Super Tuesday: Remember! Whatever state that you are in just be content, because after a little while God is going to bring you out in a mighty way!!!!

Super Tuesday: Philippians 4:11-14

Due Season

Super Tuesday: Good day beautiful happy people, today we decree this day as our "Due Season Day", God has a due season at hand for you-a time to reap your harvest of blessings!

Galatians 6:7-9.

"And let us not grow weary of doing good, for in due season we will reap, if we do not give up."

I Know The Plan!!!

Super Tuesday: God already knew the plan for your life, before the foundation of the world!!

Super Tuesday: God said just trust him in the midst of his plan for your life!!

Super Tuesday: The reason why the plan is not working is because your are too busy working on your plan, but not the plan that God has design for your life.

Super Tuesday: God says, "When you allow my plan that I have for your life to work, then you will be brought to deliverance and heal my people from their situations!!"

Super Tuesday: God already had you on his mind! He is thinking good thoughts concerning your life! Thoughts of peace not of evil!!

Super Tuesday: God has the plan for our lives! Allow him to show you that expected end!!

Jeremiah 29:11

~ Humbly Bowed~

The Test Has Ended, Know It's Time For Completion To Take Over Every Situation!!!

Super Tuesday: "It's A Done Deal

It's Nugget Time

Chapter 8

Super Wednesday

Nuggets

It's Nugget Time

Pray About Everything, But Worry About Nothing!!

You can surrender without a **prayer**, but never really pray without surrender. You can fight without ever **winning**, but never ever win without a fight.

Neil Peart

Marvel His Goodness

Super Wednesday: Lord we marvel at your goodness, mercy and compassion.

Super Wednesday: Lord, bless everyone reading this Nugget, Lord continue to be with the sick in body and mind.

Super Wednesday: Father, You are the one we go to for comfort in moments of feebleness and in times of need. Lord. Psalm 107:20 says "He sent His Word and heal them…"(KJV)

Super Wednesday: Lord you are our great physician, you drive out all infirmities and sickness.

Super Wednesday: These blessing we ask in the mighty name of Jesus, Amen.

Super Wednesday: My hope for you today is that your heart draws closer to God's heart.

Super Wednesday: God is our healer, no matter what is our sickness or disease. His word will heal us if we apply it to our everyday life!

Super Wednesday: Ps: 107:20

~Humbly Bowed~

Broken To Be Heal!!

Super Wednesday: Their come a time in your life , when you will go through Brokenness.

Super Wednesday: The broken is for you so God can get the Glory out of your life!!

Super Wednesday: Be broken by the hand of God is never going to be easy, but it will be worth it in the long run.

Super Wednesday: That is part of the process, so God can bring you into a place of healing!

Super Wednesday: Once you are totally heal then God can use you for his Glory!!

Super Wednesday: Lamentation 3:49:51

~ Humbly Bowed ~

I'm Chosen

Super Wednesday: You are a chosen generation, a royal priesthood, a holy nation, his special people, that may proclaim the praises of him who called you out of darkness into his marvelous light;

Super Wednesday: You are chosen. God has hand-picked you to be called his son or daughter and set you free!

Super Wednesday: You are called out of darkness. Responsibility is to praise the one who has made you free.

Super Wednesday: The word "response" is in responsibility.

Super Wednesday: Will you respond to this magnificent gift by accepting the call to "declare the praises of him who called you out of darkness"?(NIV)

Super Wednesday: You were bought for the highest price, for a special purpose, by a God who cherishes and loves you.

Super Wednesday: What is your response to the King of Kings?

Super Wednesday: 1Peter 2:9

~Humbly Bowed~

Overcoming Obstacles

Your life will bring all types of obstacles your way, but it's up to you to learn how to handle them in a more positive way. Life's obstacles will help you develop your faithful walk in Christ. Overcoming obstacles can be a process that may take time, but you will overcome if you stay focus and faithful to the assignment that God has given you!! Some people give in to their handicaps or allow themselves to be defeated by obstacles, but like Zacchaeus, a man who was small in stature, it would have been easy for him to stop trying to see Jesus, but he refused to give up. Jesus rewarded him for his persistence. In every circumstance have faith in God. Look to him, stand in confidence that he can help you overcome obstacles and turn defeat into victory. Do not doubt, but trust him for miracles.

Super Wednesday: Luke 19:3

~ Humbly Bowed ~

Chapter 9

Super Thursday Nuggets

It's Nugget Time

Let's Stay Motivated!

Super Thursday: There comes a time in life when you will have to motivate yourself.

Super Thursday: When you are faced with life challenges and struggles, it will seem like you are not going to make it though, just take a look back over your life, and see how far you have come!!

Super Thursday: Sometimes we think that we need people to have motivate us. No! You just have to motivate yourself in the Lord!!

Super Thursday: When you learn how to motivate yourself, then you can keep on moving forward in life!

Super Thursday: This year has really taught me, how to become self-motivated!

Super Thursday: You have to believe in yourself and that you can do it, no matter what the task may be in your life!!!

Super Thursday: Thank you God, family, and friends, for believing in me when I did not believe in myself!!! "Thanks for the push" (God)

Super Thursday: How many people feel like this was the year for them to become self-motivated!!!!

Super Thursday: I Samuel 30:6

~ Humbly Bowed~

When a man's ways pleases the Lord, he makes even his enemies to be at peace with him.

Proverbs 16:7

Thank You Lord!

Super Thursday: Thank you Lord for being an awesome Father to us.

Super Thursday: Lord, thank you for your divine protection as I slept through the night.

Super Thursday: Father early this morning we were touched by your gentle hands and that our eyes come open.

Super Thursday: Thank You Jesus for loving us, and providing for our families.

Super Thursday: Falling in love with Jesus was the best thing, we could have ever done.

Super Thursday: In his arms we feel protected, and in his arms, we will never be disconnected.

Super Thursday: There is no place we would rather be than in the arms of our Jesus!

Super Thursday: 1 Thessalonians 5:18

~ Humbly Bowed ~

Be Blessed

Super Thursday: Be blessed my Brother, Be blessed my Sister

Where this life leads you. Let me encourage you...

You can depend on God to see you through;

Keep on praying, some days my well was dry but GOD supplied.

I see you walking in favor and prosperity too.

I pray for you, you pray for me and

WATCH GOD CHANGE THINGS.

It's Nugget Time

Chapter 10

Super Friday

Nuggets

Super Friday

While meditating in prayer, the spirit of the Lord begin spoke to me saying, it's time for the people to speak to their situations so that things can begin to change. God has given you the power to speak or to prophesy to the wind and over your life. So the question is what are you speaking over your life? Positive is life - negative is death!!

Proverb 18:21

Remember you has the power to speak change into the atmosphere and in your situation!!

Keep Shinning!

Super Friday: Ye are the light of the world.

Super Friday: A city that is set on a hill cannot be hid. Neither do men light a candle, and put it under a bushel.

Super Friday: But on a candlestick; and it giveth light unto all that are in the house.

Super Friday: Let your light so shine before men, that they may see your good works!

Super Friday: And glorify your Father which is in heaven.

Super Friday: Remember! It's all about allowing your light to shine!

Super Friday: So you can make your father happy!

Super Friday: Remember! To just keep on shinning in the good times as well the bad times!!

Super Friday: Shine because you are the light of the world!

Super Friday: Matthew 5:14-16

~ Humbly Bowed~

Just Love Them!!

Super Friday: But, I say unto you which hear

Super Friday: Love your enemies, do good to them which hate you!

Super Friday: Bless them that curse you, and pray for them which despitefully use you.

Super Friday: Remember! It's so important to love people that do you wrong

Super Friday: Because, God want to bless you! He will make your enemies your foot stool!!

Super Friday: Luke 6:27-28

~ Humbly Bowed

Work It!!

Super Friday: It come a time when you will have to learn how to work the word and the gift that God had entrusted you with.

Super Friday: When you learn how to work your own work or gift

Super Friday: Then you won't have time to worry about another man work or gift!

Super Friday: Remember! Hater's (people) will try to stop your growth in the things that God has designed for your life

Super Friday: They can't because God has the plan for your life!!

Super Friday: Just remember that God is in total control over every situation!!!!

Super Friday: Remember! Even when it came to Joseph and his brother's they couldn't kill him, because God had a plan for Joseph's life!!!!!!

Super Friday: Don't sweat the small stuff, because your enemies can't kill you or the word of God!!

Super Friday: Remember! It's not you, it's the dream that's on the inside of you, that they are after!!!!!

Super Friday: Genesis 37:18

~ Humbly Bowed~

Only The Strong Will Survive!!

Super Friday: Life will breathe out all kinds of bad situations that will try to take your life away from you!!!

Super Friday: But remember when purpose and destiny is on your life, the enemy will try everything that he can to take your life away from you!!

Super Friday: You must remember that God has designed you to endure through anything that He has allowed the devil to bring your way!

Super Friday: To show you how with your faith and your strength you will always come out a winner!!!

Super Friday: Remember everything that tried to kill you taught you how to be a survivor!!

Super Friday: You have become more then a conqueror through Christ Jesus who has strengthen you in this season in your life!!!

Super Friday: Remember when you become a survivor, then you can help somebody else to become a survivor!

Super Friday: Philippians 4:16

~Humbly Bowed~

His Love Gracious

Super Friday: The Lord is gracious and full of compassion, slow to anger and great in mercy.

Super Friday: The Lord is good to all, and his tender mercies are over all his works.

Super Friday: God will show off his love toward his children.

Super Friday: He will forever me so merciful toward his children that obey his worded!!

Super Friday: We must show that same kind of Love, Mercy toward our enemies and our friends!!!

Super Friday: We thank you heavenly Father for another glorious day that you allow us to experience!

Super Friday: Psalm: 145:8:9

~ Humbly Bowed ~

It's Nugget Time

Chapter 11

Super Saturday

Nuggets

It's Nugget Time

God Is Faithful!

Super Saturday: No matter what goes on in your life, just remain faithful to God!!!

Super Saturday: When we look in the Bible we see that God was so faithful to those that was faithful to him, even in their short comings!!

Super Saturday: God is not like man because he already knows about your uprising and your down falls, but he sees your faithfulness!

Super Saturday: Don't allow people to make you miss your blessing because you are faithful to God's Words!

Super Saturday: Remember God is faithful to the faithful he will do the impossible for his people!

Super Saturday: He will always be there in every situation that will come your way!

Super Saturday: 2 Thessalonians: 3:3

Selfish Gain!

Super Saturday: While in prayer this morning, the Spirit begin to speak about how people are so hooked up on themselves and this world!

Super Saturday: But we must understand that all this is vanity!!

Super Saturday: We spend our life trying to please the world and the people, but not God!!!

Super Saturday: We must understand that everything that we have God has allow us attain them!!

Super Saturday: So What Profit A Man Or Woman To Gain The Whole World, But Yet Lose Your Soul????

So The Question Is What Is More Important You To You?

Matthew 16:26

Gaining The World System Or Gaining The Heaven System!!!

Work Together!

Super Saturday: Be tolerant with one another and forgive one another whenever anyone has a complaint against anyone else.

Super Saturday: You must Forgive one another just as the LORD has forgiven you

Super Saturday: It is so good when we can let go of the pain that someone has cause in our everyday lives!!

Super Saturday: The only way we can move forward is when you can forgive people that you know hurt!

Super Saturday: If God can forgive then we as the children of God must do the same!!!

Super Saturday: If you don't forgive then you will never be able to walk in the Blessing of God!

Super Saturday: Forgive today and receive your healing!!!

Super Saturday: Colossians 3:13

~ Humbly Bowed ~

It's Nugget Time

Chapter 12

Treasured

Nuggets

It's Nugget Time

Treasured Nuggets

Happy Holidays to all my family and friends. I must say it has been a rough year. Praying that everyone have a safe and joyful holiday. Staying positive toward any and all obstacle, that's what makes me. Hugs and kisses to the world and I meant that from my heart. From the one and only me!!

Flowing From My Heart!!

Letting Go

Treasured: Letting go of the wrong people will hurt, but embracing the right people will be much more beneficial to your life!!

Treasured: Remember God cares about the people that you allow to come into your life!!

Treasured: So trust God when it come people letting people go!!! You won't be disappointed!!

~Humbly Bowed~

Mother's Love Run Deep!

Treasured: Mothers love you no matter what!

Treasured: Mother's love you whether you good or bad!

Treasured: Mother's love will cover their children no matter what the cost is!

Treasured: Mother's love will love you through the rough times in your life!

Treasured: A Mother's Love Never Fails!

Treasured: So learn how to respect your mother at all cost!!!!!

Treasured: Mothers love will always stand the test of time,

When It Come Down To Their Children's Lives!

~ Humbly Bowed~

Bits and Pieces Nugget

Just one thing can change your life forever!!!!! God said to you that he just need one situation that would change your life forever!! So he will allowed it to make you into the man and women that you shall be!! God won't allow you be wasted!!!!!!!

From the mouth of God!

Treasure Nugget

Spoken to the man of God and asked him, "What are you going to do to the rock!!" Nothing wrong with being hungry, it's what he does when he's hungry!! It's what you are hungry for! Man shall not live by bread alone, but every word that process of the mouth of God!!

I'm The King's Daughter!!

Take Me To The King!!

Broken To Be Healing

The Inner Healing,

Is (The Inner Man Of My SOUL)...

It's Nugget Time

ABOUT THE AUTHOR

Apostle Carla Eaddy was born on June 7, 1963 to Hattie Lynch and the late Carl Lynch. She is the granddaughter of late Eddie & Willie Mae Richardson Sr. She attended Florence School District #1 and graduated South Florence High School in 1982. She furthered her education at Claflin University, Phoenix University, Florence Darlington Technical College, Dr. Sallie Dargan Bible Institute and Excellent Theological Seminary in Summerville, South Carolina, and currently Midlands Technical College in Columbia, SC.

She is the wife of Pastor Lewis Allen Eaddy and the daughter-in–law to Ruby Lee Eaddy. Apostle Carla Eaddy is the mother of three beautiful daughters, 10 grandchildren, one great grand-daughter, four God-children as well as countless others that she has been a spiritual mother to along the way. She also has six lovely sisters

Apostle Carla Eaddy gave her life to Christ under the leadership of Bishop James Hudson August 3, 1994. And in 1996, she joined *Faith Outreach Ministries* under the leadership of Apostle

Gilchrist where she served faithfully for nine 1/2 years. It was there that she preached her initial sermon titled "The Struggle Is Over".

Apostle Eaddy is blessed to be under the leadership of Bishop and First Lady Robert Christopher Brown of Sword of Truth Ministries and KFM Fellowship in Columbia, South Carolina.

On January 1, 2006, she was called by God to start *New Deliverance Faith Ministries Outreach* at 1600 East Palmetto Street in Florence, SC. On March 14, 2014 she then founded *Second Chance Faith Outreach Ministries* which is at 1141 B Ave West Columbia, South Carolina.

She has three books due to be released in 2015: "It's Nugget Time," "Faith 4 Ever Tested" and "Broken to be Healed." In her spare time she enjoys basketball and softball.

www.ingramcontent.com/pod-product-compliance
Lightning Source LLC
LaVergne TN
LVHW051131080426
835510LV00018B/2349